BIRD

BOOKS BY DON MC KAY

BIRDING, OR DESIRE

BIRDING, OR DESIRE

Poems by

DON McKAY

Canadian Cataloguing in Publication Data

McKay, Don, 1942-
Birding, or Desire

Poems.
ISBN 0-7710-5761-X

I. Title. II. Title: Desire.

PS8575.K28B57   C811′.54   C83-094172-X
PR9199.3.M256B57

Grateful acknowledgement is made to the Ontario Arts Council for its
assistance.

The author wishes to thank Stan Dragland, Jean McKay, Anne Michaels, Ellen
Seligman, and especially Dennis Lee, for help with the manuscript.

Cover photograph: Marsh Hawk, by Jean McKay.
Set in Sabon by The Typeworks, Mayne Island, B.C.
Printed and bound in Canada

McClelland & Stewart Inc.
The Canadian Publishers
481 University Avenue
Toronto, Ontario
M5G 2E9

for
John and Margaret McKay

Contents

I

just like you and me but
cageless, likes fresh air and
wants to be his longing.
Wears extra eyes around his neck, his mind
pokes out his ears the way an Irish Setter's nose
pokes out a station-wagon window.
His heart is suet. He would be a bird book full of
lavish illustrations with a text of metaphor.
He would know but still
be slippery in time. He would eat crow. He becomes
hyperbole, an egghead who spends days attempting to compare the
shape and texture of her thigh to a snowy egret's neck, elegant
and all too seldom seen in Southern Ontario.
He utters absolutes he instantly forgets. Because
the swallow is intention in a fluid state it is
impossible for it to "miss." On the other
hand a swallow's evening has been usefully compared
to a book comprised entirely of errata slips.

He wings it.

The land has been made plain,
reasoned, and made smooth with use.
Then why this restless pecking in his brain
as though its prisoner were trying to break loose

into another music?
It drives him through the back roads to those useless places
cut by creeks below the blank face of the fields:
the hairy, random
kingdom of the Great Blue Heron, dump and lovers' lane
where chipmunks animate the body of a Ford
and all shed skins, even
last summer's condoms, are reclaimed
under its gay lewd conjugal blanket of leaves.

To make a fool of yourself in the autumn woods
just leave your love at home
and walk in dying colour
knowing the reds
and yellows of her absence, letting the wind
unpick your mind
as it eases the leaves from their branches.

And when an arrow of geese
divides the sky let
your insides become
the most banal of valentines

until you see her stepping from a line of smoky hills
clothed only in Monarch Butterflies, resting,
no doubt, on her hospitable body
before continuing their long migration south
toward Point Pelee and the Mississippi flyway.

Their blood thuds fading
south, the geese
embroider their jesu joy of man's desiring way across the sky
sewing it shut.

So here we are, left to pickle bitterly
in How I Spent My Summer Vacation.
Even leftover overstuffed adjectives – munchable
bikiniclad –
now done down and bottled up
are on the prowl, tense,
dangerous as boy sopranos.

And we long for the skim of ice on the puddle, in the air
an edge, the glass knife offering itself
pure, pure crystal of madness, about to break.

Driving to the university I turn on the FM
and fill the car with Bach.
Immaculate potential: the dove-grey chevette
imagines an ancestry of silver bullets.
Back in my empty kitchen
half a cup of coffee cools. *The Birds of Canada*
roosts on a shelf while Red-winged blackbirds recompose
their meadow. The schoolbus
gathers children like an uncle, weather
occupies the morning. Somewhere slow
poetry is being tender with its alphabet.

Soon I will be erasing latin declensions left by the night class
while the dog, sleeping in the kitchen
nurtures my huge laziness in dreams
which are deep and cold
and speckled with uninhabited islands.

The freckles are leaving the landscape, toodleoo
Marian, cheerio Marge, getting
up to be
rebuffed again and
shrugging off each gust the telegrams the big
cold shoulder to fight
out of a chair at closing time into dark
air, which they flay with their hankies.

There's a kind of terror which can seize you
while you watch your kid thinking hard over her lunch
figuring out
how this   involves or becomes or affects or means
              or might be just the same as
bounding bounding through the underbrush, her grace
can clap down stillness.
Then there's a kind of sadness which can seize you
after a predator's arching act ends in squawks and flurry.
These things occur in a national park.
The cameraman's patience is also mentioned.

Concentrate upon her attributes:
the accipiter's short
roundish wings, streaked breast, talons fine
and slender as the x-ray of a baby's hand.
The eyes (yellow in this hatchling
later deepening to orange then
blood red) can spot
a sparrow at four hundred metres and impose
silence like an overwhelming noise
to which you must not listen.

Suddenly, if you're not careful, everything
goes celluloid and slow
and threatens to burn through and you
must focus quickly on the simple metal band around her leg
by which she's married to our need to know.

At the doctor's every
filament aglow she sits resisting, holding off
from panic's pure release,
milling the flood.
Her eyes
are alive with needles, their bright points
pricking and pricking and pricking.

No story dulls this edge:
        "Shoot down the Wendy-bird
        that's what the Chief commands!"
I read, under the drumroll of her heart.
The burning wheel, the gnashing mountain
this is her most difficult exploit.
I feel the effort of the breath, the indrawn
arrow, the hissing, the opening
door
the old men murmuring around the fire,
the presence, the lunging act.

Later, we surge on humming nerves
exploring (Were you scared? Not really)
the forests in us fear has opened
shooting the rapids of Vinland.

So you flew off
into your clarity of spirit.
I don't know. Down here
the heart was windy and the dark sky gulped.
Both Jean and I got parking tickets at the airport.
Did you have Doublemint to chew,
a paddler versus rapids,
against the rush of tears?
Something of this pang
is of your being too –
                          quick tooth
                          clear pool which we,
just to get a fix on,
muddy up. I suppose you realize
you left your room a bloody mess?
Also you forgot your brand new travel clock.
Listen: be deaf
to this palaver. Leave us the gift
of what you're not.

The poplars shedding pseudo-suicide notes –
not death but
female impersonation wearing thin,

tra-la.

I crunch them under my tires.

And the sumac,
haunted by her wartime childhood, dreams
how they woke and drove her to the hilltop
to watch the heart of Swansea burning
beautifully
she sets her fires along the roadside.

How am I supposed to drive with these derangements and my head
already full of Monarch Butterflies
massing on Point Pelee,
hanging in their thousands, wings folded
in the wind they look like dun dead leaves themselves their tiny
minds all reaching south in one long
empty line of poetry across the dark waves of Lake Erie?
Wind
stirs some from their branches but
they flutter, flashing orange, and recover
to grip with velvet feet:

> the concentration of Houdini
> swells toward his disappearance and return

> in Mexico.

All birds exist, including those
we only hoped to see.
The kestrels dreamt by Joe into our kitchen
perch on the fridge
and pick outrageous stories from the air.

All night huge flocks of Whistling Swans
are whistling milky ways across our dreams, the chaste
idea of arctic.
                    Angels,
protect them from the flight paths of Air Canada lest they
plunge into reality and we awake,
our hungry mouths stuffed full of feathers,
our pillows slit like bellies.

At thirteen a serpent
thrashed
about the base of her spine.
It was the snapping of wet towels in a high school locker room
locked into her loins like a cassette.
Twitching, she longed for claws.
She pulled her lower eyelids down, she stuck out her tongue –
it had a snake's head.
She screamed without sound into the mirror –
it was the soundless equivalent of a jet revving her engines but
not moving.

Bugeye, she thought, fork tongue
Twitch, she thought, and claw and curse
    and
Dammit dammit jesus fuck it's awful dammit
Dammit christ
ran through her mind from reel to reel
from leer to leer
So this was her labour's high school cheer:
        Bugeye
        Fork tongue
        Twitch curse claw
        Dammit
        Dammit
        Rah Rah Rah
Am I doing this, she thought, or being done?
Once, waiting for a boil to burst, three weeks
perhaps

and when, bent backwards in her cruel arch, she finally
                                    sprang

it was hockey night in Canada, cold
in Montreal, with hardly a wind.
And before the beautiful thunder thudded down
she was, for one soaring second
the only person alive in the whole world, swept
by her own power round the broken net
and bearing the fullness back.

L'HIRONDELLE

To be idiomatic in a vacuum
it is a shining thing!

Would I pass her by again, as always leave her standing with her
head bowed by her locker, looking like she'd forgotten the combina-
tion to everything? Could I tell her now that no one, not the most
depraved of us, deserves high school? Could I explain the way we
locked her in our lust, never speaking to her but only of, and only in
the locker room, how we turned her into a statue of desire? Could I
ask her about the feathers in her locker, taped to the inside of the
door? What would I say to that sad fabulously breasted creature,
now that my clumsiness has gnarled? Walking down the corridor of
metal doors to find you crying soundlessly, black hair pouring, the
weight of the combination lock heavy in your hand like – I see this
only now – the absence of a cock you loved. In memory I furnish
you with drapes, a used fridge and a bedroom suite ($299 at Zellers)
which I carefully arrange around you. On your cold fake marble
floor I lay this old braided rug I bought and lived on later in Saska-
toon. Here on your coffee table (slightly scratched, half price) I am
leaving my copy of *The Birds of Canada*. And listen: during the long
industrial softball double-headers of your future, be sure to look up
at the lights in case the Nighthawks may be up there

       sideslip

         downglide

    flashing their long barred wings they

                intersect with shadflies on the ad lib,

moves we never thought of, never made.

The eye observes the little rapid furl
into the foreground and the yellow
leaves beside it sing right out –
                              and moves
up river, in, above
the rapid entering
blackness
here at the heart of the canvas.

A backdrop? Yes the eye
sees how the dark sets up
the warbling rapid and the leaves'
five-hundred-watt goodbye.
But also how everything's
imperilled, how Alfred Hitchcock
appears in his own show as a waiter
waiting –
              and moves another step to feel
how textured (are you sure
we're doing the right thing how
depthed it draws us to the pool the pool which
brimsmooth for a stone or for the clean
cleaving a canoe can be the perfect
penis entering an angel, make the shapes appear
in darkness, delicate, dramatic
tangle of twigs or opulent autumn clamouring
paint me paint me as the eye
begins to know each crook and gesture of the long and
infinitely innovative
whorehouse
the velvet
closing as a lid behind.

O scenery's not scenery no more/ the stage
has shifted under us, the show
goes on
and on, beyond all ends
the eye imagines, crazy Wagner,
having killed the gods
again, refusing to finish the banquet, let's
have another sunset pal he turns
to eat the audience –
                           that's you
that's the eye, we'd better
wake up and get out of here friend,
if we can.

What I remember
about the Great Blue Heron that rose
like its name over the marsh
is touching and holding that small
manyveined
wrist
upon the gunwale, to signal silently –

                                                         look

The Great Blue Heron
(the birdboned wrist).

DUSK:

the slow
rollover of evening, the spruce
growing dense, gathering dark,
standing in pools of departure.

Take care . . . Remember . . .
we are weaving a wreath of human hair
to be left to the Huron County Museum
with a short note saying who
contributed and where they come from.

Shadows sadden.
The details of your face escape like minnows.
We become weight –

until the balance tips entirely and a bat
breaks out like a butterfly's subconscious flashing,
dancing his own black rag.

II

FRIDGE NOCTURNE

When it is late, and sleep,
off somewhere tinkering with his motorcycle, leaves you
locked in your iron birdhouse,
listen to your fridge, the old
armless weeping willow of the kitchen.

Humble murmur, it works its way
like the river you're far from, the Saugeen, the Goulais
the Raisin
muddily gathers itself in pools to drop things in
and fish things from,
the goodwill mission in the city of dreadful night.

Think of winter's starched starkness
tickled into glee: up
from roadside gravel flickering off / on /
off / on / off they swirl around the sugarbush, an old-
time movie or a laughing
manichean snowstorm.

What brings you to these well-ploughed paths of righteousness
so many flat concessions from your eskers?
What would it take to lure you to my feeder?

        silver smarties?

        Grandma's button box?

        St. Francis of Assisi?

        tears?

A PIECE OF ROSE-COLOURED QUARTZ

Watching you get dressed
again, my thought
goes searching for the words to clothe this

flowing as the sun
selects another angle down your hair along
your breast and the

underwear is hiding from you in unlikely
places and the piece of rose-coloured
quartz I picked up on an island in the Dozois

Reservoir one rain-and-windy day I walked
the beach among the
dullnesses sits now

waiting
smiling like a solid piece of
sunlight for your groping

fingers
underneath the socks.

Watch for it to happen out there on the ice:
this music they fight for.
You can feel her beside you as though poised in front of a net
circling
circling.

Christ, you'll say,
baby if you were a forty-three-year-old Montreal potato merchant
I'd be your five-iron.
I would never dissolve, in the middle of a rush, passes
coming snap snap crossing the blue line barely on-side, never
dissolve into adolescence fumbling
for control.
I would cleave
I would be your hawk
I would be silence.
Forests.
And baby, you'll say, if you conducted the Bach Society Choir
in town
I'd be a dentist's wife
straining among sturdy contraltos after your unheard perfection
longing with them to devour your wrists, your boyish wit.
I would finish your every mad flight through the defence
with deft flicks to the lower-left and upper-right-hand corners,
inevitable, the momentary angel,
your right wing.

As the first snow falls and the kids
explode with this fresh magic you
refuse
wombed up in sadness.
You will not want
to not want babies growing in your belly but
resist the current, make the air
articulate its violence on your body.
You could at least wear socks inside your boots
you asshole, but you're out to show
how this white smile is made of many teeth
how icicles are just the silver tongues of death
etc.

Listen, now. We both know this is foolish.
We know old, older, oldest,
dead.
        And yet
inside your sadness how we also find
the mute heart's answer to the sky's
pure fury flowing.

Gently haunted
it lies in repose
like a welcome-mat for imaginary
birds, or, suddenly
plural, curl into question marks.

Now, snip,
looks good to eat,
falling in soft
blonde flames

           but pausing to remember: how the sun
           slept in it warming the adventure
           in his head: we are standing beside
           a little rapid watching it
           brush its teeth, ease its sheen in sudden
           smoothness, combing
           combing until finally we
           feed ourselves to its laughter

           riding time

down to the linoleum while

outside the clouds continue and
continue like crazy Irish music unable to find the exit.

Like fingers in a mitt
we cluster against cold's
analysis,
pretending never to have heard of testicles or breasts,
resisting its finer and finer focus.

Argument from design. The dogs
are winding, wound, have webbed us in
their leashes: diagrammed: the Family
in Crisis. Observe, class, that this female child
clearly feels umbilical toward her father, who,
in turn, is drawn to some form of physical
intimacy with the black
part-lab retriever.

Meanwhile ice crystals wink
in middle distance
fading into foreground like mirage.

Offstage:
outer space.

He is conscious of his boots and dirty parka
and the superficiality of chat.
Women trundle I.V. trolleys, slowly
down the corridor, flourishing clear bags of plasma,
emblems of the perfect womb.

A more than hospital softness. Sadness
of undone beginnings. Here, he thinks
we're earlier than virgin
nakeder than nude.
Sex, a pair of shoes, is left beside the elevator.

Talk of weather: freezing rain,
could be snow tonight.
Symptoms of the world.
What can he say?
He leaves some tapes of poetry
to pour through headphones into her ears thinking

plasma

matter

feather

    energy

        chickadee

(for John McKay)

Remembering: the annual Community Chest Christmas Concert. Phone in your request with a donation, listen in bed to hear it on the radio, the small moon of the dial an extra presence in the dark as we gather toward Christmas. Jokes about the police chief and the high school principals. Choirs, bands, Billy Heward played White Christmas on the trumpet. Was it the same year someone (who?) paid twenty dollars to hear my father, a lapsed Kinsman, de da de dum his way through the Kinsmen Friendship Song while I lay thrilled and mortified *yer old man never even knew the tune let alone the words?* Might have been. At any rate I recall my father telling the story of the bird flying around the high school auditorium, fluttering wildly overhead and distracting the audience from the École Immac- ulée Conception choir singing Frosty the Snowman. By the time the Gilbert and Sullivan star tenor took the stage the bird (sparrow? hummingbird? Blackburnian warbler?) had extended its range to buzz performers. George would be singing something Irish, his voice clenched, his face set in the abstract concentration of a consti- pated man, while I see the bird flashing into the spotlight, homing on this rope of sinew in the air and veering away each time just before he flies down George's throat. The story goes that George dropped not one note or lost an ounce of poise as he caught the bird in one hand, squeezing it to death while he launched into his climax. The story leaves me lying in the dark trying to imagine how a voice might swell with heartbeats, break, and fly away, beyond the reach of radio.

Later – My father now says:

that the concert was the Kinsmen Festival of Stars

that the singer was fourteen-year-old Vincent Delasio

that the song was O for the Wings of a Dove

that the bird was a bat

that Vincent Delasio caught the bat on his third
attempt and held it until it bit him, then flung
it to the floor in pain and fury, and that later
he was persuaded to return, bandaged, and sang
again to thunderous applause.

My father will not say whether the bat survived.

Audubonless
dream birds thrive. The talking swan, the kestrels
nesting in the kitchen, undocumented citizens of teeming
terra incognita.
                    To write
their book the boy will need
la plume de ma tante, harfang des neiges,
patience, an ear like a cornucopia and at least
an elementary understanding of the place of human psychology
among nature's interlocking food chains.
                                    For the facts are scarce
and secretive. Who is able to identify
the man in metamorphosis, becoming
half-bird on the Coldstream Road? The boy reports
a falcon's beak both hooked and toothed, the fingers spreading,
lengthening into a vulture's fringe, the cold eye
glaring as he lifts off from the road: look, look,
come quick!
                    Who sits inside and fails to hear?
                    What can he be doing?
                    Why is he so deaf?

But on another night a huge, hunched, crested,
multicoloured bird, a sort of cross between eagle
and macaw, sits, sinister and gorgeous,
on our mailbox.
Now we know what happens to the letters we do not receive
from royalty, and from our secret lovers
pining in the chaste apartments of the waking world.

, chasing chance with all the moves
of swallows swirling to
connect, their physics
liquified by knives, carving and
releasing from the ice the cold
caught music of the river, stroke, stroke,
just have time to scribble you this note then
scissor and wheel syncromesh to long
parabolas of sense they pour and
drink their speed those
tossed off phrases those
sky readers those high
raptors

Another cup of coffee. Southern Ontario
surrounds this kitchen like well-fed flesh.
If I had
a cigarette right now I'd smoke it like an angry campfire
burn it into the unblemished body of the night.

Lonely is a knife whose handle fits the mind
too well, its oldest and most hospitable friend.
On Highway 22
a truck is howling for Sarnia or London.
In my garage
the aging Buick is dreaming the commercial
in which he frees my spirit into speed while an eagle
                in slow motion
beats applause above our heads.

Another cup of coffee.
Two years ago the wolves took shape
in Lobo Township, lifting the tombstone of its name
to lope across these snowy fields
                            between the woodlots
                      spectral
                                legless as wind, their nostrils
wide with news of an automated pig barn
waiting for them like an all-night restaurant.

Shot, their bodies wisped away, their eyes
stubbed out.

Waking JESUS sudden riding a scream like a
train braking metal on metal on
metal teeth receiving signals from a dying star sparking
off involuntarily in terror in all directions in the
abstract incognito in my
maidenform bra in an expanding universe in a where's
my syntax thrashing
loose like a grab that like a
look out like a
live wire in a hurricane until

until I finally tie it down:
it is a pig scream
a pig scream from the farm across the road
that tears this throat of noise into the otherwise anonymous dark,
a noise not oink or grunt
but a passage blasted through constricted pipes, perhaps
a preview of the pig's last noise.

Gathering again toward sleep I sense
earth's claim on the pig.
Pig grew, polyped out on the earth like a boil
and broke away.
                        But earth
heals all flesh back beginning with her pig,
filling his throat with silt and sending
subtle fingers for him like the meshing fibres in a wound
like roots
like grass growing on a grave like a snooze
in the sun like furlined boots that seize

the feet like his *nostalgie de la boue* like
having another glass of booze like a necktie like a
velvet noose like a nurse

like sleep.

1.

Next to nothings.
If we grew such bits
of laughter on our bodies we'd enjoy

a finer intimacy with the air,
a tax break.
We would learn to catch

the animal of wind but shed its teeth, we'd be
the voltage regulators of its huge
guffaw.

Consequently we redream
the dreams of prehistoric fish, in which
our scales become the seeds

of intricate well-tempered
forests shading hair by zippered
hair, impossibly

composed.

2.

The nightmare. He is walking his favourite trail; it's early and the dew is heavy on the grass. As often, the paper mill faintly taints the breeze. He sits down by the railway cut, peels a banana. Across the tracks a warbler he doesn't recognize flits into a pine. He raises his binoculars but the bird seems to   be changing, as if putting on fall plumage in the space of a few seconds. No, not changing but moulting, feathers falling in a yellow white and bluish snowstorm under the tree. Now plucking out its feathers angrily with a suddenly hooked beak. Grown much larger and its red eye glows like a brake light. The bare patches no pink flesh but leathery-looking, like lizard-hide. Now the bald bird is glaring at him, moving towards him, somehow crawling up the binoculars' eyebeam, wingless; he drops the glasses and flees back down the trail. The sky has darkened, as though a nictitating membrane slid across the sun, the air acrid, biting at his throat with every gasp finally reaching the cabin but   the door is locked. Fumbles for his key, feeling the thing slide through the air behind him. The keys all unfamiliar. He prepares to smash the door with an ax, wakes up.

What a headache. Pulls on his socks and staggers downstairs to the bathroom, opens the medicine chest above the sink. The thing slumps on a shelf, slurping up a livid soup: eardrops, Murine, wart-remover, toothpaste, vitamin E, Dettol, Dristan Nasal Mist, the 222s he needs. It is grinning through a face vaguely Judy Garland but wrinkled and pouchy as an aging boozy writer, an incredible grimace calling muscles never used before. Between thin lips a poisonous forked tongue flicks. He reels back, grabs the door, wakes up. For real this time, but drained. You could have knocked him over with a feather.

A movable ghetto,
bickering on the feeder: suddenly
a Blue Jay, they
scatter to the currant bushes and
regather: then to
jabber back, hardy
and unkillable clichés
chirping to beat the band
(while deep inside cacophony
their group mind takes the microphone:
non, je ne regrette rien, le grand
trombone du vent the wintry
dicta, enfin let the
space between our voices be my nom de plume).

ADAGIO FOR A FALLEN SPARROW

In the bleak midwinter
frosty wind made moan
earth was hard as iron
water like a stone

Sparrows burning
                    bright bright bright against the wind
resemble this item, this frozen
lump on the floor of my garage, as fire
resembles ash:
                    not much.
A body to dispose of,
probably one I've fed all winter, now
a sort of weightless fact,
an effortless repudiation of the whole shebang.
I'd like to toss it in the garbage can but can't let go
so easily. I'd bury it
but ground is steel
and hard to find. Cremation?
Much too big a deal, too rich and bardic
too much like an ode. Why not simply splurge
and get it stuffed, perch it proudly on the shelf
with Keats and Shelley and *The Birds of Canada*?

But when at last
I bury it beneath three feet of snow
there is nothing to be said.
It's very cold.
The air
has turned its edge
against us.
My bones

are an antenna picking up
arthritis, wordless keening of the dead.

So, sparrow, before drifting snow
reclaims this place for placelessness, I mark your grave
with four sticks broken from the walnut tree:

one for your fierce heart

one for your bright eye

one for the shit you shat upon my windshield
while exercising squatters' rights in my garage

and one to tell the turkey vultures where your thawing body lies
when they return next spring to gather you
into the circling ferment of themselves.

And my last wish: that they do
before the cat discovers you and eats you, throwing up,
as usual, beside the wicker basket in the upstairs hall.

How come you don't see more dead pigeons?
Because when they die their bodies turn to lost gloves
and get swept up by the city sweepers. Even so
their soft inconsequence can sabotage a jumbo jet
the way a flock of empty details
devastates a marriage.

Someone down the hall is working on an epic cough.
Another makes it to the bathroom
yet again, groping past my door. All night
the senile plumbing interviews itself: some war or other.
The faint sweet smell of must.

Along the ledges of the parking garage they flutter
wanly as the grey blue residue of nightmares.
Softness of bruises, of sponges
sopping up exhaust.

City poets try to read their tracks along the windowsill for some
announcement. Such as our concrete palaces
have the consistency of cake. Such as
Metropolis of Crumbs. Such as
Save us, Christ, the poor sons of bitches.

Let's admit
the heavy lusts of entropy.
Let's eat rich
illicit proteins of despair.
Let's cultivate a taste for the appendix.

    Let's each of us
    anoint a duck with oil
    and make comical home movies of its antics.

    Let's arrange to buy the final Whooping Crane
    and eat it fried, Kentucky style.

    Let's watch the nesting instinct of the Bald eagle weaken
    shells grow thin
    its brilliant simple mind go dim with pesticides.
    Let's tell cuckoo eagle jokes, e.g.
    "Why did the cuckoo eagle forget where she laid her eggs?"

    Let's train kamikaze starlings.

    Let's plan the street map of Necropolis
    let's have statues of everybody.

Let's learn our own
dead weight.

A MORNING PRAYER ENDING WITH A LINE BORROWED FROM HOLIDAY INN

May the poem
waiting at this morning's end
be the mouth which fits its
bite, its
tongues of sun
moving inside the ice mist may it
gather from refractions, frosted
spruce trees nearly vanish in white
air, a vapour trail goes
rose and shreds
slowly, while a treeful of starlings, speckled and
oily as comic book germs or high school wiseguys, mocks
the whole dumb enterprise –
                              words!
may you find repose in your
attention, as my mind
lifts off from the business of scraping the windshield
and folds around the seminal
idea of her body, left
snoozing in its holster, fellow guests
of time the best surprise is no
surprise.

Eyes opening into an oblong of pale
light lying on the wall
obliquely like the shadow of the
shadow of a door, and ears

into the chipper chat and
here we go folks music don't you hide your love away that
drifted over from his brand new radio and

downstairs how acutely
angled sunlight broke
open in the kitchen like an egg and

Joe was eight. Gifts
hummed upon the table, space
arranged itself around.

A Blue Jay
snapped up to the feeder and snapped
off again in two
pop-bottle-opening moves, crisp
blue and white and
of the sky and snow the way the
oblong light was of the wall:
                                    it seemed
that light led day through openings
of one kind and another:
mouths

mouths which remain as smoothnesses in mind
where oftentimes the action is as skating on cement.

Who says the dead have no imagination?
The outdoors
holds its pose. In roles
of this and that appear
their ghosts, furred and still
as harp seal pups in photographs.

Breath grows mossy, visible
cliché. My car
also wishes it were dead, repeats
were dead, were dead
before it kicks and runs.

By ten they are slipping
softly off their wires and branches,
tender panties dropped
for no one in particular.

May my last words be so apt,
so accidental.

Something stupid and relentless, possibly
a giant teething baby
gnaws the eaves and corners of my house

howls in prespeech, turns it over and
over in clumsy hands it waa and
waa and wants
to stuff the long
dark tunnel of its appetite.

Open the door and step
inside the madness of Vivaldi, inside a mind
dispersed in particles,
antibodies that attack with tiny teeth, abrade
erase efface
all features, fill

all holes until the space between the earth and sky
becomes a vision of the final egg, the
earless eyeless ovoid
heaven of the dead reclining nudes.

MARCH SNOW

The snow is sick. The pure
page breaks and greys and
drools around the edges, sucks
at my snowshoe every heavy step saying
fuck it, just
fuck it, softly to itself.

It fails the toothpaste test.
In fact, it makes me think of dentists
frowning, the sag along the jawline as he
hmm as he
mutters something to his nurse
whose complexion's turned to cottage cheese
from too much Harlequin Romance.

So is it possible to
fix a person to her place, to pin her
like a name tag to her
self.
I missed
the atomic fission of her yearning till I looked back

bang into a fiery lake: the snow
suicidal with desire, wearing
his image like a poster of the movie star
she dies to be   the sun
simmering in her flesh her
nerves her burning
bedroom eyes

too bright for mine.
Beside the house scared earth emerges

frawny with sleep, imagines
the atrocity of tulips thrusting up
dog-penis red and raw.

THE ROUGH-LEGGED HAWK, THE WATCHER, THE LOVER, THE BLIND

A Rough-legged hawk hovering
above the field beside the old folks' home
arrests the watcher in his car.
No lover of the field

        say, Henry, 90, soaking weak April
        sunlight into his plaid-rugged knees
could know it hair scalp follicle and
scruff with the intensity of the rough-
legged hovering hawk

        whose black wing patches
        impossibly still hanging in the air
        are staring straight through into earth's

        subconsciousness.

But Henry, lover of the field, having no
power to stop time or penetrate or
throw the world to neutral
has accumulated field on field on field
and mixed its faces in his memory like a cocktail –

        that stump that was the elm like an
        umbrella, the brambled ruins of the shed, that
        soggy patch, that winter when the drifts
        were higher than his head and – stand up sonny –
        higher than yours too.

And so the watcher throws himself into l'envers
and takes the tactics of the blind. Casually,
carefully, he slings his tarp among the apple thorn

(crabapple jelly, '55), the wreckage of a flying dream in which
he incubates, accepts
contingency, hinged as his lawnchair, elbows
firmly on his knees to balance the binoculars he's

focussed on thin air
                    attends
the rough-legged uncles of the wind.

Migratory Patterns

Long scarves of sleep unwinding through the house, the dark heart
rides its deep
cathedral breathing, sinking
               slowly trailing fin de siècle fingers
as a child behind a rowboat, 2 A.M., no place
open to buy smokes or numbly roost, the dark

heart sideslips, grieves all early closings everywhere, as when
at eight he dove into the black, aware he'd
have to learn to swim

before he hit the water, turn the
heart to muscle, fist himself
against the world, où sont les

restaurants nocturnes d'antan the dark heart knows
the sneakiness of winter, maple celebrates the first
tinge of arthritis, death begins to blossom, all the hatchling hawks

unfold: sense pressure: weather
tightens and they drift beat soar
and harry south, the Marsh hawk

tilts, a rufous breast, a white patch
flashing, stoops upon its prey, pressure, Kestrels,
trim and lethal, Sharp-shins, Red tails,

funnelled by the Great Lakes into concentration, genius
swells toward catastrophe along
Lake Erie, wind in the northwest we watch the blank sky
burst, aboil with, someone breathing christ the Broadwings,
                                hundreds,

more, soar toward us swift and still and
still without one wingbeat turn

and spiral even higher, climbing in their kettle so far into blue
                                                    the eye
is sucked up through the lens into its element

and blinded
            pitched past all capacity

II

shifts in seeing, gifts,
suddenly your eyes where ears had been
you're watching from the wings:

the osprey in full scalloped stretch above the creek that
buckled, folded on his flight becoming
plummet, turned into the very gravity
each feather is the delicate
repudiation of:
                a shaft the dark heart dwells on, in,
                a friend writes
of a Great Blue Heron hunting in the moonlight, stalk and bend
and stab along the ordinary beach, sewing a scene
past dreaming from a silent, silver, innocently
violent domain:
                to write on air, to brood on marble eggs,
                to bear such traces, nearly
                legible

and when winter hung
invisible shirts up in his closet, pushed
his shaving brush to one side leaving space

for who knows what cosmetic or what
iodine of time, when angels
lost their tans the dark heart,

rinsing his razor, watching
icy light reflected in the mirror zing right
through his head and resting nowhere growing

nothing seek its home in snow
the dark heart
hoping loneliness could be the fridge he held an egg,

imagined summer protein sleeping
zoo zee zoo zoo zee among the white pine, hum
you gunner from the infield, how about
(thinking of his friend's song, sad
beyond the blues) a fried egg sandwich (3 A.M.)
on plain white store-bought bread
                              and how about
a tape of Emmylou right now to help
defray expenses, how about

abruptly bounding into this old town
filled with sin the woofing of the dog
who died last spring, accidentally

taped with Emmylou, a sudden
pocket of pure outcry

III

Distinguished from the twerp,
which he resembles, by his off-speed
concentration: *shh:*
                    bursting with sneakiness
he will tiptoe through our early morning drowse
like the villain in an old cartoon, pick up
binoculars, bird book, dog,
orange, letting the fridge lips close behind him with a kiss.
Everything,
even the station-wagon, will be
delicate with dew –
bindweed, spiderweb, sumac,
Queen Anne's Lace: he slides
among them as a wish, attempting to become
a dog's nose of receptiveness.

Later on he'll come back as the well-known bore
and read his list (Song sparrows: 5
                    Brown thrashers: 2
                    Black-throated green warblers: 1)   omitting
all the secret data hatching on the far side of his mind:

                    that birds have sinuses throughout their bodies,
                    and that their bones are flutes
                    that soaring turkey vultures can detect
                                        depression and careless driving
                    that every feather is a pen, but living,

        flying

On a branch in the yard the Cardinal
is coloratura
                Noble in carriage
                Beautiful in plumage
                Amiable in disposition
                Excellent singer
                Best of birds
says the *Eastern Bird Guide,* 1906.

But the cat, the most
exacting of his critics, seems unimpressed
abstracted lounging on the grass smoking a cigarette.

The cat gives nothing he is wrapped up
in himself.
Only the practised eye observes under his sheen how he
coils the snakes of his body
into a single
pent
sentence

writing a bird guide
with black-edged pages.

was the shadow of another cat
he couldn't catch, though he slid through his days
without abrasion, unsurprised, surprising
everybody else, appearing
at your elbow as a sudden
hole in your attention yet
bored with his good looks and flowing
into motion he attacked his sleeping
sister licked cigar ash chased the squirrels once
he tried to screw a pumpkin surely
there is more to life.
Even in repose his eyes were cigarettes of wrath
burning into the feline condition
which enclosed him like an egg –

until at last he was surprised by a car
on Cheapside Street and his life turned
jerky as a slideshow.
Now we look him up in memory under lithe:
flexible limber pliant supple:
stiff with attributes.

Some claim forepangs in their shoulder blades, others
that the light grows dim, or else
(too many westerns) that air
winces to a single long drawn minor chord.

Serene, décolletés, unflappably
they circle, oval
and parabola,
    an elegance, a laziness
that masks the naked ache of appetite
as distance masks the outrage that their heads are wounds.

Calling nothing, building no nests,
they lay their eggs on rock.
Everywhere they see through to the end (he shoots
her lover, dynamites the mine, leaves town),
eliminating spring as so much juice.
The Great
Souwesto Desert offers its hors d'oeuvres.

LONGING:

a term for radical unwinding of the heart, e.g.
an angel
calling his dog, a cardinal
whistling in the poplars plucks a dangling
heartstring in his beak and
flies off somewhere, carelessly
                    in Welsh
                            across the clothesline

                                    bleeding into the trees

Silence tastes
when something snaps
                    killdéer   killdéer
shaken as salt

a pen   poised a beak
attacks its shell   a mind   a mind

a mind might give itself away to the wind, as it
seethes through the dead reeds by the creek or as it

grieves in the barn carding combing itself through cracks
into long fine strands and soughs

out through the field I have
nothing whatever to wear and last year's grasses
sigh behind like faded lingerie
                              a mind sows
gives itself away to the wind
inscribes in air this vanishing
wingbeat

Home from the hospital she sits
in the kitchen on the wobbly pressed-back chair
among familiar flowers.
Across the walls their tendrils
lock back into pattern like a chain-link fence
around a playground –
                              aching space
accepts her.
O my
says Lee Remick in *Wild River* as she
walks through the tiny cottage she is destined
doomed to share with Montgomery Clift, o my
o my.

·

Tonight her ears are
(now that we notice) slightly pointed,
elfin, poised
to feed the smallest mouth with listening.

Real life arrives like painless migraine.
Thought-fronds poke
unfurling into air, the warping
floor boards groan against their nails
                                        creatures
of the small room time allows inside itself
the embassy from space

·

this is rich this is oysters this light lays
gold bricks right across the kitchen.
She sits on the wobbly pressed-back chair and lets it
sweet-talk through the afternoon, remembers
in winter how it
knifed, not as an assassin or a surgeon but an
aesthete, somewhere in Africa,
precisely
delicately paring fruit.

1.

When we get close the barn goes
schizophrenic, thoughts
                    panicking from windows, swirling then
            banking swirling
        more slowly, settling and
    returning to their
nests.

2.

After God invented the swallow he sat back
satisfied.
At last,
the aeronautical bird.
This, he thought, is going to be one hell of a surprise
for them mosquitoes.

3.

With unpremeditated blue
                        d
                         e
                          s
                           p
                            e
                             r
                              a
                               t
                                i
                                 o
                                  n

                                    h
                                     a
                                      i
                                       k
                                        u
                                          moves they are
too small to play in the NHL

4.

Under a Red tail's wing we are all
on the same plate
slowly rotating –

             while the snickersnacks of the air,
the swallows cut and thrust carving smaller more
surprising spaces

        birthdays

           other bits of death.

5.

the cut back wing the
edge the forked tail the impetuous
gesture of a child that leaves you standing
razor in hand
searching the face in the mirror for obscure deserving

Here's to your good looks and the neat way you shit
with a brisk bob like a curtsey, easy as song.
Here's to your song, which,
though "neither rhythmical nor musical" (*The Birds of Canada*),
relieves me of all speech and never deals with what is past,
or passing, or to come.
And, as a monument to the sturdy fragile woven
scrotum of your nest,
I hereby dedicate baseball.

Far hum of highway
                    undersilence
                              spatter of rain
the big spruce heave and sigh like ships:

              think of all the nests and
nests in progress up there swaying twig by
straw by string by bit of rag
                         and of our own

coagulations   from inside
the manic voice of playoff hockey, close-shaved, naked,
furred by the tuning up of fiddle and guitar
                         while underneath
the kids are blowing eggs:
                         noises from our rich
and slithy pre-existence.

Gliding in long caress the last
half mile to the pond
the Whistling Swan films high points of my life dissolves
the sweet arc of my jump shot to the smooth
glissando of your body on the hillside sliding
braking down the long back of the air he brings
imagination brimming to its edge before,
with startling black feet braced,
our ache resolves to water.

IDENTIFICATION

Yesterday a hawkish speck
above the cornfield moving
far too fast its where are those
binoculars sharp wings row row row the air above
the Campbell's bush it
                              stooped and
vanished
          Peregrine
                    I write it down because

I write it down because of too much sky
because I might have gone on digging the potatoes
never looking up because
I mean to bang this loneliness to speech you
jesus falcon
fix me to my feet and lock me in this
slow sad pocket of awe   because
my sinuses, those weary hoses,
have begun to stretch and grow, become
a catacomb my voice
would yodel into stratospheric octaves
                              and because
such clarity is rare and inarticulate as you, o dangerous
endangered species.

among the spruce: Bach
would put this evening on the cello
and chew it.
You would feel the long strokes
bite and sweep, everything
curve away, arching back
against the bow.
You would know the end before the end
would understand the Red-winged blackbirds calling
konkeree   konkeree   the sexual
buzz   the silver
falling whistle hanging from the top spines of the spruce
like tinsel.
You would dwell in imminence.
You would arrive home empty

covered with burrs

ready

Some things can't be praised enough, among them
breasts and birds
who have cohabited so long in metaphor
most folks think of them as married.
Not only that, but
when you slide your shirt (the striped one) off
the inside of my head is lined with down
like a Blackburnian warbler's nest,
the exterior of which is often rough and twiggy
in appearance.
And as the shirt snags, hesitates, and then
lets go, I know exactly why he warbles as he does,
which is zip zip zip zip zeee
        chickety chickety chickety chick.
The man who wrote "twin alabaster mounds"
should have spent more time outdoors
instead of browsing in that musty old museum where
he pissed away his youth.

Among humans, only
baseball gloves and vulvas, organs
who embrace their guests in velvet,
can rival my dog's nose.

Say hello. Pat his noble head.
Feel him lift your aura gently
lead it through frescoed passages
down to the furry boudoir of his heart.

Sweet Georgia Brown.
This is where your glands hang out,
this is where the band makes
gravy, thickening the mix
with woofs and recollected howls, *'f you
don't like my taters how come you dig so deep,* saliva
burbling down the long trombone.

More than the shortest distance
between points, we are
the Stradivarius of work.
We make the meadow meadow, make it
mean, make it yours, but till the last
insurance policy is cashed in we will
never be immune to this
exquisite cruelty:
             that the knots in all our posts remember limbs
they nested and were busy in and danced *per-*
chic-o-ree their loops between,
that the fury of their playfulness persists
in amputated roots.
Remember us
next time the little yellow bastards lilt
across your windshield. No one
no one is above the law.

again.
Sparrows were blown past the feeder
like little ladies past their bus stop.
The cat
sat on the fridge and complained.
Sniffles, coughs,
a sad retreat to rule.

These words are the coat
the stripper borrowed from the cop.

erasure:
        waits
for the next call,
notes that are the air bunched,
shaped by body and released
cleanly through a ruthless beak
        (touching there upon the true
        obscenity of opera: lips)
     arrives
home sensitive and empty swallows
skirling in his head he takes his
pen and stabs each
member of his alphabet . . . o my fury   look
         this merchant dies for you

"The name 'Sparrow hawk' is unfair to this handsome and beneficial little falcon." *The Birds of Canada*

1.

unfurl from the hydro wire, beat
con brio out across the field and
hover, marshalling the moment, these
gestures of our slender hostess,
ushering her guests into the dining room

2.

sprung rhythm and
surprises, enharmonic change directions simply
step outside and let the earth turn
underneath, trapdoors, new lungs, missing bits
of time, plump familiar pods go
pop in your mind you learn not
principles of flight but how to fall, you learn
pity for that paraplegic bird, the heart

3.

to watch by the roadside singing *killy killy killy,*
plumaged like a tasteful parrot,
to have a repertoire of moves so clean their edge is
                                        the frontier of nothing
to be sudden   to send
postcards of distance which arrive in nicks of time

to open letters with a knife

IV

All day tiny scratches tsip
tsip tsip
         tseet
entice him from the trail.
            Where are they?
      Try another angle
      (brambles, deadfall).
Show yourselves you little buggers: shiny
three-leaved plants.
          Now at owl-light
most remain as teetsa   teetsa
weesee weesee weesee – Black and white, Yellow,
possibly Bay breasted warblers, Redstarts –
question marks he broods on
warmed by the fire and scotch
               till later,
one ear still open for
           hoo hoohoo
he finds himself surprised to think them
orphans of one huge lost populous
imponderable thought.

Next morning, as he pokes his
fuzzy head outside the tent
           the Yellow warbler on the picnic table cocks
           a dark eye, pecks
           a crumb,
           flies off.

"In our dance philosophy we say: Think before you move."
The Techniques of Isadora Duncan

Watch me.
This is how I walk
softly and carry a sharp stick
lightly as a paintbrush. This is how I
mill the slow
momentum of the earth how I
turn its turning to my
reaching how I
swirl up to a point
releasing silent pings among the birdsongs.
And this is how I wear my maidenhair
to stroll the slope, how I invite
your eye to know the smoothness of my limbs'
articulations, elbows, armpits
backs of knees
lovelier than which I think that you will never see.

SOME EXERCISES ON THE CRY OF THE LOON

(for Rob and Carole)

Write a book about it
and tear out all the pages.
Drop your rake and jump into the ditch, then
climb out and continue raking. Show them
intermittence is more elegant than suicide.
Caution: do not think these things while driving.
Instead, let memory replay the leap inside you
while you brush your teeth. Observe:
for that split
second at the break your reflection vanishes
to drink the crystal whisky on the other side.
If souls had pockets
we could bring it back in bottles, sit down
on the porches of our minds
and sip it (Jesus) carefully, like drinking otters
licensed by our own L.C.B.O.

must send its words to ballet school under the Red Pine
where they will learn stand and stand and
lift and cradle with the wind

must teach them roost and watch
and lose your wits with grace
swimming smoothly in the populace,

so that when the poem wants
rumour of the patient
animal of evening, all its words
will be as secret agents in the field

incunabula

empty and foolish, eyed and eared

The passing cars caress   trucks
thud   leathered in air   messageless
strokes of a masseur. Each river
is its slim green sign, then a wry smile
squirms beneath the bridge
that staples it in place: the Nith,
the Grand, the Credit, the Rouge, the Ganaraska, Trent and
Moira, to the Salmon cutting into deeper country
with the gesture of an arm
half-raised in farewell:
                              illegal exits.   O,   once
upon a time we park beside the Salmon,
sit for a moment in the awe of what we are about to do,
take down the canoe from the roof and,
with one wave backward,
paddle off into a beautiful B-minus movie.

In the dim unwritten folklore of the heart
they are the soft grey sisters
muting the cries of their brother, the Great Horned Owl, to
woe
    woe
        woe for every victim, calling,
recalling the Passenger Pigeons who were much as they
but rosy-breasted, brighter-eyed, *amoureuse* and bigger.

POOL

Early deepshadowed pool we come
on tip-toe to your whispers of fish, to flick
these flies, sol-fa,
                        touching
exactly on your surface.

The real flies hang
ardent in air
full of their own small destinies
vivid with undelivered news –

but wait:
let us enter with ritual
flexings of elbow and shoulder, let us know your
delicate contingency as virgins vaguely
deeply stirred would know

that somewhere in their sleep
the sleek trout lurk.

Granite, the last word,
sun's drum,
one hundred thousand tombstones in the rough.

No shadow. Obvious cicadas buzz
the way crazy people talk too loud:
God is clean.

If he could hear the minor
song of the White-throated sparrow
blues could begin
                    he could
steal a penful of permanent blue-black ink
and pivot at the edge.

If his sense of humour goes
he knows he will know nothing
and too well.

PAUSING BY MOONLIGHT BESIDE A FIELD
OF DANDELIONS GONE TO SEED

Bygones, the many moons of the moon
catch and concentrate its light:
                          listen

                          the car ticks as it cools
                          rustle

                          absence of owls
                                    everything thin, silver
                          virgin as Ophelia's lingerie
adrift
            no more
afternoons of running butter.
Gossip is dead.
            Your next breath
triggers ten million peccadilloes.

Endless copulation without climax.

Heat beating with the flat side of the blade, earth
cracking in ghastly grins it can't
it can't quit now
                    the toilet
sweats a swamp into the bathroom.

Meanwhile the sun,
a South African surgeon, is interviewed
on TV, explains
procedures, tolerances, cardiac
arrest, the statistical
chances of major morbidity.

Our hero hoes in the garden feeling
futile, an orderly at Geri-Care he
feels the flesh
dissolve   the bones
cry out for final whiteness.
His mind
steps to one side   sees
grasshoppers flick through the space
his body was.

He wakes that night
the air's grown hands it
picks them all up like an egg and
                    thunder cracks so close
the windows shriek the mad
aunt has escaped is running through the house –

the rain breaks hard like canned laughter.

The afternoon turned Spanish with sleeping lust.
The air seethed and darkened
measled with bees, black
but ardent holes like burnt out eyes.

Someone had politicized the peasants.
Dozing with power they slowly
grew around the queen, ripened
on a rose bush into teeming dark
forbidden fruit:
               our heads
grown numb and heavy, felt unborn
poems hump and stir and
drag their slimy half-formed bodies from the cells
to stare out, furious and stupid, from our pupils.

Half-past midnight. Your new watch
has been keeping perfect time for five full hours:
you're thirteen: a fact we have massaged
with scotch and old-time fiddle music
till it glows inside like dubbined leather.

Friends are leaving, having
thickened up our air with smoke and
bawdy ancient English folksongs
a capella. The balloons
begin to detumesce.

Let us consider the plumbing
its great sadness
its profundity.

Now time is ready to present
the last gift: tickets
to its sedimented years (the scarlet
fever birthday, catching fireflies,
the incredible pierced ears affair, and
in the next to the bottom layer, just
ten minutes old your fierce black eyes establishing
their snug caves in my brain)
                        but the dog
like the appendix of the party, crazed with fun, goes
crashing through a window for the
fourth time in his brief
but action-packed career.

is falling a certain way through the dining room window
I want to lapse in speech on the balcony, sprawl
in a lawn chair watching
how the shadow shoves it up the hospital wall until
it winks so long from the top floor windows, float
words like maple keys on thick
and sleepy air.
I want memories that germinate, the things
we both thought when your mother
fell and cut her knee that time I helped her from the car,
the fight in the hotel in Edinburgh, other
fights and hotels we have known   I want
the caterpillar to stop eating the thick
leaf of the evening   I want
the kids to sit and reach inside themselves
to wonder at the seed they were.
I want to spread the shed years on us
as a mulch   I want
unfoldings in my head like fast-growing plants in an old
Walt Disney movie about spring, do you remember?
Do you remember?
Simply because of this
I am bugging your ass in the kitchen
disparaging the dishes, slamming cupboards, flicking
bits of old no longer titled movies at you like the
foam from the detergent just to make you say
for christ's sake let's go have a beer
on the balcony instead of –
                            clip clop
I'll uncap them
and we will.

Sing to me softly.
Hum.
Let your lullaby be muzak: preverbal
polysyllables.
I've got to think about Rilke, Rex Morgan, the proper depth
to plant peas. Can't afford
to wind up in the red.

Underneath I feel you
writing on my verso
busy as Karl Marx in the British Museum Reading Room
dreaming of the day

the sun lies in the grass like lust
the cicadas stop
     suddenly
I wake up
as a spray can full of Easter 1916, turn

to the white wall of the afternoon
and publish your long wild in-
decipherable river

astonishing my strawberries

bequeathing sticky feet to flies.

VICKY

For centuries we've been sitting in the sand, your words
are blubbing as a one-holed can
of juice.

Your thoughts
are blotches in the air, useless placentae.
The landscape is as smeared, daubed as the walls
of a cave.

Vicky, you've lived in that squirrel skull nine years eating
and excreting your own mind –

              your ripped red dress your clairol mother oh
              Henry bar father your unmade bed a dish falling
              off a ripped red grin your unmade mother oh
              Henry bar bed your falling off father his ripped
              red dish her clairol bed your falling off grin his
              unmade dish her oh Henry dress your clairol
              falling off unmade oh Henry ripped red –

                                                  purée
you return to with such multiplied disgust.

No wonder you take a vacation.
No wonder you detach – beautiful, a White-throated sparrow –
from your bunched self in the sand.
I sit holding your body, your bad dreams until you come
                                      back for them
while your pain slinks away to its own unknown arroyos.

Everything is full but she
keeps pumping on the inside
chintzing up the outside till her month becomes
a regular rococo whorehouse in an expanding economy.

Back and forth salaam salaam the sprinklers
graze and pray on plush
carpets of grass, beer becomes sweat, the heavy
air surrounds, mothers us to immobility, the mind
melts, the elements
slump, four fat uncles in their lawn chairs, while the flesh
well the flesh just ambles into town to get drunk
                                        with the ball players.

We knew this ripeness and we knew
her smiling, solitary
reaper.
The shiver slid
beneath the sunburn with the fatal
rightness of a shift to minor key:
she loved him, she dressed up in her gypsy best,
she left.

CONCERTO FOR VIOLIN AND ORCHESTRA

Poised
coiled in his power
he hears the pitterpat of running
thirty-second notes before they reach the ear and

enters with surprising lightness,
tight, in full
possession of the tortured

sinews of his instrument, whetting and
spry across tentacled roots he picks up
rustlings in the woodwinds, fresh

news from the many nesting
warblers, gathering their twigs
twittering under a sky in which the only troubling speck

is the Red tail
musing, moving among paths of air, letting
earth slide underneath him like a menu, then

to perch: poised again
until it hooks on his eye he lifts off
nearly casual he takes out knives and forks the orchestra

swelling up to meet him, the conductor's elbow
cocked to drive the hunger
home to the small upsurging

flesh in the grass he flashes in
with brisk efficient strokes he seizes it
and eats it
             shrieking into melody

Owl owl owl.
He finally, late that summer, spots a Great Horned Owl at
dusk in a dead elm by the fence line. Big, blunt, clumsy
as a tombstone, she suddenly
                              swoops across the field –
lyric of ending.

No one stands a chance.

•

But in daytime can be made ridiculous as exiled potentates or night-
mares. When crows discover a dozing owl they will often gather to
caw in huge numbers, driving it to some other territory and dimin-
ishing its efficiency that night. Occasionally they fail to distinguish
between nocturnal owls and those who eat lunch. They flock and
caw around an unfamiliar Snowy Owl, recently arrived from tun-
dra, who wakes, discovers herself in a fancy southern restaurant,
spreads wings like a linen tablecloth –

•

To film this nest of Great Horned Owls we had to erect a scaffold for
our blind close to their tree. (Shots of scaffolding and floodlights
being carried through the bush.) Then we set up spotlights on three
sides. By this time the owls have too much invested in the youngsters
to object to an audience (shots of scrawny owlets like brainy bespec-
tacled three-year-olds) or demand a contract. Looks like supper
tonight is Meadowlark which Mom has brought home from her
shopping expedition. (Dipping beaks into the yellow breast as
though into a yolk. Indrawn ahs.) Well, nature has her darker side.

Actually, the owls are great conservationists because they eat their prey entire (a whole wing disappearing down an owlet) including the feathers, fur, bones and beaks. Later they disgorge the indigestible bits in neat pellets.

•

One night darkness finds its voice outside his window: hoo hoo hoohoo. At first he lies and listens, letting an iceberg float through his mind. Then goes to the window and scans the spruce and maples, but its shape will not detach from shadow. Pulls on jeans and boots, runs out on the lawn, but the owl has heard the screen door and shut up. Somewhere up there two huge eyes devour his image. As we know, owls eat their prey entire, including jeans, boots, wallet, watch and delicate intelligence. Later they disgorge the indigestible bits in neat pellets, which are saved and used to build the parthenon of nature's darker side.

Focussed on his own front lawn. Every year thousands of Canadians are reported missing. What happens to these people? What are the police, social agencies, poets and clergymen doing about it? How can you tell if someone you know is about to become missing?

•

Later deeper into dark he is once more pulled from the covers. This time moonlight fills the yard, soaking into the bricks beside the window. Why he unbuttons his pyjamas, why he steps out onto the porch roof, he can't say. Moonlight, radiant and cold as x-ray, saturates his skin. Hoohoo surrounds him, pulls his name into its interrogative. He creeps, peering, to the roof edge. The eavestrough is so cold his toes clutch. Well, nature has her darker side. He soars off into night, trailing a long black ribbon like a loosely scribbled signature, left to hang from branches and hydro lines, and corkscrew smartly up his neighbour's silo.

·

Because the feathers of an owl are soft and fluffy he is able to fly silently, caress the air. His victims have no warning but the sense that *something's missing,* into which they fall. If the shadow of an owl should cross a poet's roof he wakes up, wild, often with moths in his pyjamas, his pecker pointing to the north star.

At the edge of firelight
where the earth is cradled in soft

black gloves filled with unknown hands, where
every word is shadowed by its animal, our ears

are empty auditoria for
scritch scritch scritch rr-ronk the
shh uh shh of greater

anonymities the little
brouhahas that won't lie still for type
and die

applauseless,
humus to our talking. Listen

while they peck like enzymes, eat
the information from our voices, scritch
and whip-poor-will and peent, o

throat, husked in smoke and finely
muscled, play these on your juke box

ohms of speech.

Perky still, asway
tossing the thistle's white hairs to the wind,
he's not so vivid as he was. The fuse
from eye to heart burns slower and his name,
emerging into mind, fits strangely –
Goldfinch –
          with this brownish grey and
slightly yellow at the throat and shoulder, wing-barred bird.

The brain roots for its words, essentially
a pig. Not quite smart enough
to not get fat.
We woke up this morning to the shape of sharpened hearts,
the fallen poplar leaves' "insignia" on the tent.
Sweet birds,
resist.

Yesterday there were voices in the constant
causeless swell of Georgian Bay,
grumbling under and against its cliffs,
articulating caves, coves, shelvings,
oracles in mumbo jumbo breaking
boulder into pebble into
          syllables of sand
             which trickle through my fingers.
Now, just as we pack to leave
two tiny hallowe'ens excite the cedars: Redstarts: moving

Some of these poems appeared first in *Fiddlehead;
Harvest; Impulse; Tics; Applegarth's Folly; Brick;
Eclipse; Toronto Life;* and the *New Oxford Book
of Canadian Verse.* "Alias Rock Dove, Alias Holy
Ghost" was first published as a broadsheet from
Dreadnaught Press.

Several poems are reprinted from *Air Occupies
Space* (Sesame Press), *Long Sault* (Applegarth
Follies; Coach House Press), and *Lependu* (Brick
Books).

Lightning Ball Bait, which Coach House Press
published in 1980, is still in print. Twenty-five
poems from that collection belonged thematically
in *Birding, or Desire* as well; they appear here by
courteous permission of Coach House Press.